THE WONDERFUL KINDNESS OF THE STRIPPER'S ASS AND OTHER POEMS

A Marvelous Book of Great Novelty

By His Lordship
Apollo Polyhistor Starmule

About The Poet

Apollo Polyhistor Starmule is the premier Southern novelist/poet launched two centuries into the future. Arriving in the late twenty-second century with a case of the ass and a case of cheap beer, his only communication with the world he left behind is thru a telepathic poetry connection he established with a twelve year-old idiot savant who is pursuing her master's degree at Princeton. Thru this connection he authored the astonishing novel *UNDO THE WINTER: The Odyssey of Sonny-Bob Culpepper*, which defines and largely created the new genre called Speculative Mythology; the book of poesy *AH, MAN! A Slim Volume of Poetry*; and a short nonfiction visionary metaphysical book with Pagan overtones called *CRUCIFIXION AND RESURRECTION: A Pamphleteer Speaks*.

He is devoted to the moral elevation of humankind thru the evolutionary reclamation of all aspects of human nature, uniting heaven and earth in each human being. For only when the sunlight of the soul touches the soil of our passion can the sacred rose of compassionate lovingkindness begin to bloom.

A PUBLICK SERVICE MESSAGE

Well, you could spend your money on some good eats and on a couple of theater tickets, but that stuff's only good for one evening, and then your money's gone and your lady may not even cooperate with your designs, leaving you practicing your "one-handed embrace" in solitary.

But Apollo Starmule's books will never let you down, and with proper care will last for a very long time, as they are printed on archival quality acid-free paper. You can experience them again and again amid the chuckles and groans of your ecstasy, for there are scenes in some Starmule books that may prompt you toward that old "one-handed embrace" while stimulating your "chuckle factor" with their foolishness.

Of course, Apollo Starmule's books appeal to the ladies, too, though their methodology for embracing themselves is somewhat different, somewhat more refined. Plus, a woman in ecstasy is a pleasant vision of loveliness, but we would not make the same statement with regard to a man. Are we prejudiced in favor of women? Well, we suppose we are.

Apollo Starmule gives you the best of all worlds for one relatively low price, so BUY STARMULE FIRST!

*The preceding was a publick service message brought to you by the Buy Starmule First! Committee, which is not affiliated with any other group you've ever heard of.

This Goode Booke Published By

Satya Yuga Books™
Asheville Weaverville Nacogdoches Tokyo

To The Lady
With The Blue Star On Her Ass

The Wonderful Kindness of the Stripper's Ass
And Other Poems: A Marvelous Book of
Great Novelty

ISBN 978-0-9763230-4-4

Cover Designed by Chris Master

Interior Design Muddled Thru by Apollo
Starmule

Nevertheless, We Do Encourage You To
Purchase Multiple Copies Of This Tract For
Distribution To Your Church Library, Sunday
School, Or Drinking Buddies.

This Product Would Also Make An Important
Statement As A Part Of Any Vacation Bible
School Curriculum, Or Any Other Curriculum
Devoted To Moral Virtue And Sexual
Awakening. Thank You For Your Patronage.

preface

I've never seen any difference between poets and strippers, or between poets and prostitutes. When they are properly tapped into humanity's emotional processes, both poet and sexworker are the artists and architects of human psychology, portraying our most stimulating and redemptive visions of our human natures as they are, and as they are becoming. For the sea of emotion and of visioning that upholds and stabilizes and fosters the growth of our humanity is a beautifully shifting spectrum of poems which are created in various ways.

The professional stripper, for example, shifts into poetic mode and actually *becomes* a poem when she is inspired onstage. She becomes the vibrating poem of her own fullest, most divine human beautifulness, and she is the transmitting agent for the poem of herself to her appreciative audience. She will be well-rewarded financially for becoming this poem, and for transmitting herself as poem, into the tendered awareness of the supportive audience, whose own poetic conscience is somewhat quickened and redeemed by her joyful sacrifice. With this enhanced appreciation of the beauty of their own conscience, the members of the audience will be inspired to live fuller lives more in tune with the beauty of their own human natures.

I consider sexwork to be a good career so I am happy to be a poet.

In the future, I doubt if a person will be considered qualified as a psychologist or psychotherapist unless they have first spent time as a sexworker. The unlived life is not worth examining!

* * *

The first time I had a religious experience in a church was in Columbus, Georgia. It wasn't officially considered a church by the authorities, but it was the best church I'd ever attended. Officially, it was considered a strip club.

I'd been raised a fundamentalist Christian and was busily shucking the dirt of that unholy nightmare out of my aura when I was cleansed and liberated and partially redeemed by the strippers of Columbus. I had just begun to consider myself a Zen Buddhist, and after visiting the strip clubs I realized that my ideal temple would be a combination of a Zen Buddhist temple with a strip club. This was long before Paganism had come into the open to any substantial degree, and I don't know if I even knew the term Pagan, or that people who considered themselves Pagan even existed. So I did not realize that I was feeling within my body, emotions and soul the rebirth of that refreshing, liberating, ecstatic, natural religion called Paganism.

Since that time I have been affiliated with some Pagan groups, and though I presently do not formally identify with any group, I am always born bodily aloft on the energy of the natural religion which everyone's body, emotions and soul naturally resonate to. I live in a place of gods and goddesses; not in the dry, stale academic sense of those who have chosen to limit themselves to intellect and scholarship, but in the sense of the fact that the gods and goddesses are real forces of Nature, constantly evolving and interacting with humans and with the greater environment, and I know them personally.

The woman to whom this book is dedicated and who the title poem is about has always remained in my memory, even though I only "knew" her for one night a quarter of a century ago in a Memphis strip club "temple". She knew perfectly with her whole being how to be a woman, and that the function of Woman is to serve as a revealer of Truth thru Beauty to Man, who then goes out and creates a religious form to attempt to "ground" and exemplify that Truth. He presents this form--be it a ritual, novel, hymn or whatever--as an offering to the Lady who inspired him. The offering of flowers to women is a reflection of this practice.

And all these religious forms prove that human beings are fundamentally good, until the forms are misunderstood by succeeding generations. Perhaps humankind will soon mature enough to cease from misunderstanding, and learn to hear the voice of love that lies behind and resonates with every living form.

I don't remember for sure whether this Memphis dancer was actually a Yankee, as she is described in the poem, but she was certainly different. She was a Force of Nature who understood perfectly how to be a woman. I guess this could be one definition of a goddess.

Anyhow, if you are a lady who works, or who has ever worked, as a stripper or other sexworker, give yourself an "Atta girl!" and pat yourself on the back, then strut off into your day to inspire a man with a refreshing vision of Truth thru Beauty; at the very least he will probably be moved enough to put some cash in your collection plate. And he might just write you a poem.

NEW TESTAMENTS BY APOLLO
STARMULE

*UNDO THE WINTER: The Odyssey of Sonny-
Bob Culpepper* (fiction)

*CRUCIFIXION AND RESURRECTION: A
Pamphleteer Speaks* (nonfiction)

AH, MAN! A Slim Volume of Poetry

*THE WONDERFUL KINDNESS OF THE
STRIPPER'S ASS AND OTHER POEMS: A
Marvelous Book of Great Novelty*

And more releases are prophesied, so stay
tuned!

THE WONDERFUL KINDNESS OF THE STRIPPER'S ASS AND OTHER POEMS

A Marvelous Book of Great Novelty

By America's Best-Loved Poet
Apollo Polyhistor Starmule

Apollo Starmule

THE WONDERFUL KINDNESS OF THE STRIPPER'S ASS

Pale, luminous twin moons
perfectly rounded with muscle
she sees only the nighttime
and reveals not her pale face
to the blushing day,
with its rose-petal sweetness.

A Yankee girl, in Memphis
who knows how to make
the South rise again
and is well-paid for it;
her twin-made buttocks
glowing before my alert eyes,
eyes which should be bleary
after thirty-seven beers
but they are raptly fastened
upon her glowing tail assembly;
let it be said
that the Yankees not only ravaged the
    South,
but provided for the reconstruction of its
    Spirit,
once strip joints became common.

BAPTISM

I receive you into the warmth
of significant virtue
and join my psyche to yours
my soul to yours
my body to yours
acknowledging you as a source
of inspiration to me
my sister
in the brotherhood of the water,
the brotherhood of warmth
compassion
of supportive love
of emotion that transcends itself
to find itself wandering among the gods
aware of its human divinity
for the first unrestricted time.

JESSICA

Your name, like a rhythm of light
dances across my tongue
ripe with meanings I hold dear
advancing into old age, young age
flowing back upon me
the rhythms of time are not so wide
that I cannot see you
standing upon the shores of the present
where you seem to always be
as my heart, that timeless organ
opens wide to you again.

SIF

You do not compleat me
and never will
but I find your company pleasant.
I am compleat in myself,
just as you are
and together we make a unit
that assembles itself for a while
thru the compatibility of complementary
    vibration
the knowingness of all our molecules
singing happy songs of *nowness*
with futureness taking care of itself
while the past is but a fading misty dream
dissolved by some special magic
contained by our awakened bodies.

Apollo Starmule

1950

Hey, cat--you feelin' beat, man?

Naw. I ain't feelin' beat. Just a little ragged,
is all.

I heard that, kitty cat. I be one hell of a
doggy dog, man, but I ain't got enough spice
no more. You diggin' me? I ain't got no
spice. Gimmie some spice and I'll be right
there with ya.

Doggie dog, ain't you got no sense? Nobody
got no spice no more, man. Ain't nobody got
it. Done exhausted the spice. Now we got
to start usin' the fuel, man. You know, the
real stuff.

Kitty cat, I ain't got no real stuff--

Shut yo mouth, doggy dog. Everbody's got
the stuff, man, but don't nobody know it.
Listen: what's the sound of one hand
clapping?

Don't know, furry kitten. I never heard such
trash.

Look in the mirror, doggie dog. Chase your
tail.

NUDE FOOD

I like her sometimes
when she is nude
food
for my whole body,
whether thru a quick glance
or urgent touch;
sometimes one is enough,
sometimes the other is required.

Some girls look better nude
than clothed
and she is one of these.
I like smelling her,
putting my nose against
her big lips
as I'm on my knees
and she likes being smelled.

She has big hands and feet
and sits around nude a lot
so I can smell her.

Apollo Starmule

THE ESTABLISHED POET

I look forward to signing my name
on their shiny young asses
(and upon their teats, for I
am a vast fan of teats)
with a felt-tipped marker
in Barnes and Nobles
from coast to coast,
and maybe even in Brentano's
if I ever get up thataway;
maybe Barnes and Noble doesn't allow
a cooler full of beer
to accompany poets
on ass-signing tours,
but for me they'll have to make an
    exception.

Apollo Starmule

DRIED LEAVES I READ ONLINE

I read some dried leaves
about Whitman,
devoid of juiciness were these leaves,
devoid of light they were.

These dried leaves,
these decaying leaves,
dealt with the poem
"To A Common Prostitute"
which is one of the holiest scriptures
ever published.
It is a psalm
that would make a child weep
and shows an acceptance
that could only come from a child's heart.

Yet the dried leaves spoke
and tried to cover the voice
of Whitman
with their own tired crackling.

You cannot understand Whitman
unless you understand God.
Whitman understood God,
and wrote with the voice of God.
Whitman was an intimate of God,
he was God's child.

Yet the dried leaves
(as dried leaves always do)

Apollo Starmule

tried to cover Whitman's flower.
But Whitman's perfume still rises,
splendid, delicious
and it always will,
until the dried leaves become flowers
themselves.

Apollo Starmule

THE SPIRITUAL SYMBOL OF THE COMING MILLENIUM

When I look at a nude girl
I see my reward for being alive
for being a human being.

Nude girls civilize us
and without them
our spirituality would wither and die
into a stale form of fanaticism
that fears the beautiful.

Symbols of death do not resurrect me;
nude girls have always resurrected me
and as long as nude girls exist,
humanity will have a chance
to be free.

Apollo Starmule

I SALUTE THE NEWS MEDIA

Immoral, pompous, moralistic bastards
taking the place
of the Puritan ministers of old,
covering up your own fears
by fostering massive outbreaks of perversion
(such as your enthusiastic initial support
of the Iraq invasion / conquest)
which reinforce, and even create
terror in the fevered imaginings
of your audience,
who then grasp at more media "news"
as tho' they were grasping at one more fix
from the most stale and insidious drug
the earth has ever seen;
we've gone from being a global village
to being a global crackhouse
with you coiffed media-masters
pushing the drug
of giving in
to your own ridiculous fears,
the drug of psychic terrorism,
as you help your brothers
in the formal terrorist networks
try to cover up the sweetness
the earth automatically provides
to those of innocent conscience
who understand that the only true news
is the tapping into the love
at the core of the earth
that lies hidden from those

Apollo Starmule

who have let you media-masters
keep them from discovering
the truth of their own hearts.

NIGHTLY NEWS

The stale long stare
down the length
of powdered nose,
emphasizing some new point
(or reemphasizing some old point)
of restriction
that you seem to feel you have the right
to impress upon the Publick
thru the medium of fears about their health
or physical security;
oops, don't want to lose control
in this wide world which seems out of
    control,
but we already have lost control,
so what's next?
Huh?

Apollo Starmule

AWAY IN A MANGER

I remember that time
around Christmas
when I was a bum, standing
in the Wal-Mart vestibule
where the payphones were
waiting for a call from a friend
dressed in Wal-Mart rags
that I had bought
from another Wal-Mart
in another town
years before.
Years and years before.

So tired, usually, but on fire
with spiritual emergency this Christmastime,
    this Crucifixiontime
a burning zeal that would not put me down
and made me introduce myself to a young
    lady
also waiting in Wal-Mart's outermost
    chamber;
she was seventeen, I think;
I kissed her hand at some point,
for we had a good conversation going;
she was alone, had fought with her mother
and left home, but her boyfriend
was supposed to meet her at this Wal-Mart
and take her to where he lived, wherever
    that was.
She needed the phone, too, to talk to him,

and once I talked to him for her.
He did not seem overly thrilled
by this unexpected visit from his girl,
but was not hostile, either, just maybe
a little lethargic. A nice
enough chap, I guess, in his own way--
I do not remember if I stank that holiday
    evening
in my bumwear,
but the girl did not seem
to think so,
and I liked her
and suggested she join the military,
but this was before the conquest of Iraq
proved that America could not be trusted
    with a military.
I hope she ignored the advice
from an old and outwardly decadent cold-
    warrior.

At one point
a mother and her small son
passed us by
in this Wal-Mart vestibule.
They had come, I guess
to buy some of the good things
that Wal-Mart sells.
"Mama!   Mama!" the little boy cried
    excitedly,
pointing at my rusty-long beard,
"It's Santa Claus!"
"No, that's not Santa," she mumbled

31

dragging her son away from me,
a look of barely-subdued terror in her eyes
"Santa has a white beard."

How would you know, bitch? I wondered.

SHIVA ON PARADE

If you've been somewhere they can't
   imagine going
they won't welcome you back
they will spit at you
as if your roaring flame
were but a candle
that could be quenched
by the unkindness of animals.

Apollo Starmule

A FEARFUL JESUIT TAKES A STEP, ALBEIT STUMBLING, IN THE RIGHT DIRECTION

Young girls, ripe with fearful lesbianisms
puckered lustings, yearnings
for the elderly frankfurter,
that hotdog of desire
which mostly nods sleepily now
while occasionally trying to make up
for lost time,
unplumbed opportunities
of frankfurter youth
wasted on jesuit education
trying now to extricate self
from homosexual embrace
to secretly offend doctrine
by chasing young skirts;
no priest should *ever*
be interested in girls.

Apollo Starmule

PAGAN BABIES

I am a person much like you are
we both have a religion
whose tongue is secretly spoken
by the mass of people in every land.
Every sort of person
knows our sacred language;
we lie together
and the movement of our bodies
gives the alphabet to our sacred language
our muted chantings rising and falling
with the sweet rhythm of breathing
into one another's lungs.

The rest of the world
may pretend not to know us,
yet in their secret hours
they return to their true religion
which is our overt religion
of unifying human nature with the divine
thru this respectful communion.

BURL, THE ROMAN SENATOR

"You can live off beer,"
Burl declared,
and I had no reason
to doubt him,
nor any desire to,
as I myself was
an aficionado of beer.
But I didn't want
to live off beer alone.
I think Burl may have been
an alcoholic.

Burl was a construction worker
from up in Caintuck
but I saw him as a
Roman Senator,
the bright toga flashing in and out
before my eyes
as he helped with the reconstruction,
the remodeling
the reincarnation
of a famous Nashville department store.

Burl reincarnated as a construction worker
to serve as midwife to a department store.

Who says one hand doesn't wash the other
as the wheel of incarnation
carries us slowly beyond restriction.

Apollo Starmule

WISDOM OF THE RED

I smelled it
the scent of burning leaves
leaves that could be chewed and spat
or inhaled from a bowl
great undertakings from a bowl of peace.

I lowered myself
embracing the ground
and worked my way cautiously
to the crest of the hill.
Peering over
I saw the return
of the short-horns
like an ocean they covered the prairie
an ocean of white dreams,
for there were no longer dark short-horns.

I caught my breath
on the fragrance of the burning leaves
igniting spring in my lungs
with a mysterious power of faded longings
and fresh new dreams.
At once lifted, but sad
I lamented the loss
of the world of the dark short-horns,
but the freshtide of spring in my chest
brought me to the white ones
and by the time I got there
there was joy in my step.

Apollo Starmule

BOOSHIE-POO, ARE YE DEEF?

He refused to hear
downplayed the significance of minorities
refusing to hear their voices
the left-leaning trees were not part of his
    forest, anyway
didn't vote for him
he won without them
felt he didn't need them
shook his head and turned his back on them
forgetting his role as forest-warden of all the
    trees
allowing no voice of peace to complete its
    delivery
his own voice shriveled
and dying inside him,
fettered by old karmic ties
snapped back by those ties
like a rubber band
he wriggles out of compassionate
    conservatism
to return to the old duel.

Apollo Starmule

CHAINED-UP MELODY

He's dueling away our rights, you know
Booshie-poo
Ashcroft, his henchperson
a chilly wind blows from Washington
cooling the warm embers
of internal debate
and inquiry
getting lists of books
you've read
surveilling your computer
ready to pursue you
at no provocation
because of your race,
religion
or taste in literature
pushing you to the edge
of the cliff
that leads to the
fall of conscience
when you stop thinking,
stop feeling
stop reading unsanctioned literature
and never protest
when a stranger is dragged away in chains.

Apollo Starmule

BEAUTIFUL DEVIL

Beautiful Devil
a princess among your kind
red horns and red plastic thigh-high boots
against pale naked flesh,
robust with beauty
you awaken me from dreams
of angelic kingdom
where sex is a gift
between equal souls;
you bring me to a world
where sex is an offering
to the robust flesh
that houses those souls;
and now I see
that you are necessary
and desirable.

Apollo Starmule

TO FILL THE DEEP-OCEAN CAVITY

Electric currents whispered to me
made me aware of her nature
one whose toes have not known my kisses
of appreciation for their beauty
whose cavity remains unfilled
by the boldness of my thrusting manhood
whose lips remain dry
to the taste of my moist and sloppy tongue;
a salty pond between our bodies
we depend upon the electronic
for whisperings between us;
and I am no longer one
for plunging headlong into some new
    adventure--
developing a sense of stability
is important to me now.
Only when I can carry
this sense of stability with me
and can kneel with it before her
will I allow myself the inspiration
that will come of touching lightly
the deep beauty
she carries within her body.

Apollo Starmule

THE BODY IS SACRED

The spiritual excitement
of a living human body
is like electricity.

She lay naked on our altar
a great bed with fresh sheets
purchased especially for this virgin moment;
she was prepared to receive our worship,
having just incorporated into the awareness
    of herself
what it meant to be worshipped,
to be a woman bold and brave
sacrificing herself upon her own passions,
a sacrifice alive with joy.

She lay relaxed, yet poised
her power to excite
shining forth from her own eyes;
she commanded this moment
she was our Goddess
and we worshipped her.

Apollo Starmule

THIS IS AN UNTITLED POEM WHICH APPEARS IN THE SECOND HALF OF MR. STARMULE'S ASTONISHING NOVEL OF SPIRITUAL REDEMPTION, *UNDO THE WINTER: THE ODYSSEY OF SONNY-BOB CULPEPPER*

There was a bright light
and I looked for the source of the light
and found a soul-strong woman
sexual and secure
a shamaness, seer
a peerer into mysteries so divine, so deep
that had I followed her all the way back
I would have become lost in her
I would have drowned in her
yet I wanted to drown in her
and I still do.

II

Placing my body on the ocean for her
as sacrifice and sacrament
upon her glistening tongue
deep and wide I am called
by a lady of the sea
whose essence lives in Kentucky
in a temple of bright flesh
she has sacralized, sanctified
thru the union of all she is
I smile in happy death upon her

Apollo Starmule

joyous amid the wave churnings
lost in deep contemplation
of her eternal mystery,
made null to all I was before
yet positive with her attractive mystery
I dwell with her
and she recognizes me within her
and her face there, just above the ocean
smiles with me
amid whisperings in a sacred language
humans have always known
and must never forget again.

NOTES

You may use this space to write your own feelings regarding the journey you have just experienced. The reading of a book is less a journey thru the author's feelings than it is thru your own. The author is merely a mirror-maker; his book reflects your own thoughts and feelings, thus making you more aware of yourself. What do you see when you look into the mirror? The probability is that you are Beautiful, which is why I have called the existence of the mirror to your attention.

www.ingramcontent.com/pod-product-compliance
Lightning Source LLC
Chambersburg PA
CBHW061757040426
42447CB00011B/2342